BEYOND PORRIDGE

DISHES FROM INSIDE WOMEN'S PRISONS

ISBN 978-1-914603-49-5 (Paperback)
ISBN 978-1-914603-50-1 (EPUB ebook)
ISBN 978-1-914603-51-8 (PDF ebook)

Cataloguing In-Publication Data: A catalogue record for this book can be obtained from the British Library.

Published 2024 by
Waterside Press Ltd.
www.WatersidePress.co.uk
enquiries@watersidepress.co.uk

BEYOND PORRIDGE

DISHES FROM INSIDE WOMEN'S PRISONS

Edited by

Maria Adams, Jon Garland, Vicki Harman,
Daniel McCarthy, Erin Power and Talitha Brown

With a Foreword by Jon Watts

☒ WATERSIDE PRESS

Contents

About the Editors

Maria Adams is an Associate Professor in Criminology at the University of Surrey. Her main research interests focus on prison life, families, and identities. She is a lead investigator on the Economic and Social Research Council (ESRC) funded project 'Doing Porridge' on which this book is based and which looked at food in women's prisons.

Jon Garland is a Professor of Criminology at the University of Surrey. His research interests include hate crime victimisation and perpetration, prisons and prisoners, far-right groups, racism in rural and isolated areas of England, policing, and racism and disorder in football.

Vicki Harman is a Professor in Sociology at the University of Reading. Her main research interests centre on family life, food, social identities and social inequalities.

Daniel McCarthy is Professor of Criminology at the University of Surrey. He is also Co-Director of its Centre for Criminology and has conducted research across fields of policing, punishment and youth justice.

Erin Power is a Lecturer in Criminology at Liverpool John Moores University. Her main research interests focus on prison life, prison arts, care and gender. She has also worked as a prison arts facilitator and prison-based family practitioner.

Talitha Brown is a Research Associate at the University of Glasgow. Her research interests include young people, lived experiences of the care system and prisons.

We dedicate this book to all the women in prison who trusted us with their experiences, feelings and cherished moments.

All royalties will be donated to the Women in Prison charity.

Women in Prison is a national charity that supports women affected by the Criminal Justice System and campaigns to end the harm caused to women, their families and our communities by imprisonment.

Foreword by Jon Watts

This is a recipe book like no other. In the pages that follow you will be taken on a unique culinary journey by some of the women who are currently being held in the UK prison system.

Something I always noticed during my own time in prison is how human beings carry with them an incredible ability to adapt. Reading through some of these recipes I am truly amazed at the creativity and genius that it takes to create such recipes.

During my own time in custody I developed a love for food and cooking, and it has since become a passion and a successful career. The one thing I often remember is how the quality of prison food affected the whole morale of the prison community. If the food was bad then the morale was bad, and vice versa.

This book serves as a testament to the transformative power of cooking. Beyond the steel bars and concrete walls, these recipes carry with them stories of redemption, strength, and the resilient human spirit.

The authors of these recipes invite you to join them in breaking down the barriers that often define them, one creative dish at a time.

May this cookbook inspire you to look beyond preconceived notions and appreciate the resilience and creativity that flourishes, even in the most unexpected of places.

June 2024

The Author of the Foreword

Jon Watts turned his life around by becoming the first person ever to win Bronze, Silver and Gold Duke of Edinburgh Awards while serving time in a young offender institution.

After learning to cook in prison (and working in one of Jamie Oliver's restaurants) he went on to become a cooking social media influencer, celebrity chef and private and corporate events caterer.

His *Watts Cooking: Deliciously Simple Recipes to Inspire Home Cooks* was published by Meze in 2023 and his second book *Speedy Weeknight Meals* by Bloomsbury in 2024.

Introduction

Make Real Bread?

Pre
St

What do I do with this?

s for the
pboard ?

Home Baking

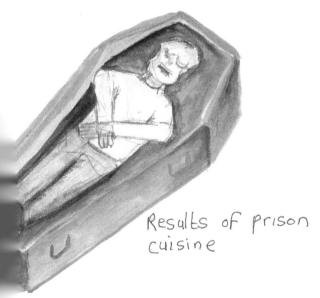

Results of prison
cuisine

Previous Page:
Death of the Prison Cuisine
Betty

A t the time of writing, there are currently 3,219 women in prison in England and Wales, representing about five per cent of the overall prison population (Gov.UK, 2024). The 2007 Corston Review of the state of women's prisons described women in prison as experiencing multiple forms of vulnerabilities, with needs different to men. Corston identified that prisons are designed for men by men, and that there needs to be greater regard for women and their circumstances. Many women in prison are likely to commit non-violent crimes such as non-payment of TV licences, something which has significantly risen across the years. Many women are victims themselves, experiencing forms of domestic abuse and drug/alcohol addictions. Issues of mental health and suicide are still critical in the women's estate, with many dealing with traumatic experiences from their past. Women's experiences in prison are distinct from men's and comprehending this provides a deeper understanding of gender-related issues on inequalities, poverty, mental health, and adversity.

Food in prison performs a vital role in the physical, mental and emotional wellbeing of people in prison (Her Majesty's Inspectorate of Prisons, 2016). It provides a way of structuring the day and is often pivotal to interactions between those who are incarcerated, staff and other prisoners. Furthermore, food practices and eating habits play a crucial role in the construction of gender, ethnic and cultural identities. Therefore, cooking in prison for women can be described as a valued experience that is distinct from the outside, and from the men's prison estate. Furthermore, it enables women to have opportunities to learn culinary skills, gain a sense of independence as well as undertaking activities that resemble limited aspects of domestic practices. Cooking is an example of both survival and agency that contributes to wider experiences of prison life — to the sensory experience of being imprisoned and having less control over aspects of life that people on the outside often take for granted, such as deciding what to eat and when to eat it.

Despite the importance of healthy eating being increasingly recognised in many areas and institutions of society including schools, hospitals and care homes, severe budgetary constraints operate in relation to food in prisons. In England and Wales the budget for prison food is just £2.71 for the three meals and drinks per person per day. This is less than the cost of a typical lunch for a primary school-aged child — which is around £2.80 for one meal (*The Guardian*, 2023). The prison regime also provides food at times that people out in the community would find unusual — with breakfast packs being delivered in the evening before they are due to be consumed the next day, for example. If eaten in the evening as is common, this can lead to a long wait before the next meal. This provides a hint at the importance of preparing one's own food in prison — so that people can have more control over what and when to eat.

Due to the restrictions in prisons, many women found creative ways to cook in many spaces in prison, and therefore this book is a collection of dishes from women across four prisons in England and Wales. Drawing from the two-year Economic and Social Research Council funded 'Doing Porridge' research project that examined women's experiences of food in prison, these dishes have been collated from the women who took part in the project and shed light on women's journeys before and during their sentence. The aims of this research were;

- to explore the preparation and consumption of food in prison;
- to identify the social and cultural influence of food in prison; and
- seeing food as a value and a social currency.

This study collected data from focus groups, observations, artwork, and interviews. The women were from a diverse range of backgrounds, ages, and disabilities, and this also included a variety of both short and long-term sentences. Overall, there were 108 women who took part in the research project.

Each prison taking part in the study was distinct from the others, and this included features like the architecture, food provisions on offer including self-catering, horticulture, butchery, with one even featuring a farm. In this, there are many issues related to the relationship between the experiences of women in prison and the role of food. These dishes were cooked by women in their cells, communal kitchens or on the wings, and some women had access to kitchen utilities including microwaves and toasters. Often prepared in areas of limited space while making the most of resources available, ingredients are often an approximation and able to be substituted if necessary due to shortages — sometimes leading to new, creative dishes. Whilst this book will shed light on the opportunities in cooking, it is important to argue strongly that these were often rare and incredibly challenging due to the strict restrictions in prison. Women in prison would often use the canteen sheet (which is a list of additional foods available to purchase) that gives women some autonomy to customise their foods and to make their circumstances more liveable. Women would depend on cooking in their cells and would often utilise kettle cooking, making a range of dishes including kettle curry.

These dishes represent further conversations around the relationship between food and inequalities, accessibility, and affordability. Many women voiced tensions that existed before prison around the cost of food and its availability to them and their families. The women's testimonies spoke about the relationship between mental health and eating habits in prison; for example, one woman related her experience of being in an abusive relationship that led to her fearing that her food would be contaminated whilst she was in prison. Similarly, other testimonies highlighted that there were traumatic elements of eating food in prisons including concerns about being served smaller portions at mealtimes through to fights breaking out in the canteen area due to arguments about food.

For many women, the food they experienced from the servery was often high in carbohydrates while choices were limited, and addressing individual dietary needs was often found to be problematic and too bureaucratic. Cooking their own food provided a source of agency and often a connection to social identities prior to incarceration, including ethnic and cultural identity and performing their family role of cooking for others.

In this book, we will narrate a range of testimonies that contribute to the background to these dishes and will also provide information on how to cook each dish. All these dishes are a testimony to the struggles, resistance and loneliness of women in prison, yet they also embrace 'celebratory' moments that the experience of being in prison can also provide. This collection has been split into three themes that explore:

- the role of kettle cooking;
- the memories evoked from *home*, including how cooking became a purpose for women to embrace their personal identities, either culturally or socially; and lastly
- the way women celebrated significant moments like birthdays, religious events, or anniversaries.

The images presented have been captured in the art procured from the workshops developed from this project and displayed in a highly successful exhibition hosted in 2023 in partnership with Koestler Arts (a charity dedicated to encouraging people in the Criminal Justice System to participate in the arts).

We hope that this book invites new ways of thinking about food in women's prisons and celebrates the creativity of the ideas displayed, whilst also giving voice to women's critical thoughts about the current regime and suggestions about how things might be done better.

It is important to remember that these descriptions come directly from the women themselves — they are their authentic words, not a sequence of steps to follow. We hope that they give you an image of the kinds of creative ways that they can be resourceful and caring to one another through the creation of these dishes.

2 YEARS OF 23 1/2 HOURS IN CELL

LOCK UP
CASSANDRA

Kettle Cooking

Previous Page:
Cutlery
Jenny

> *Massively, it's been an absolute life saver, even though that's, that makes life, much, much easier, and a kettle in your room.*

Kettle cooking has been a core part of cooking in cells. Indeed, kettles are a popular piece of cooking equipment in both men's and women's cells to cook an array of dishes that are suited to cultural, social, and dietary preferences. Using kettle cooking was not officially allowed or encouraged in prison but generally neither prevented nor sanctioned. Defining kettle cooking is easy as it's reflected in the title itself: it's simply cooking done in a kettle. Furthermore, kettle cooking is a practical tool for women in prison to be creative when cooking and to exercise aspects of individual identities. Some of the dishes from kettle cooking include curries, stews or even midnight sweet snacks. The most well-known dish is noodles cooked in a kettle, as noodles are accessible and affordable from the canteen.[1]

Other ingredients included breakfast items like eggs, porridge or even pasta. Women identified that kettle cooking was an asset to stave off hunger or an alternative option that was different from cooked meals. Many women described this type of cooking as innovative or creative which for some felt like an achievement. Porridge was ideal for women as a replacement to the breakfast served to them. Breakfast usually consisted of packs that were based on cereal, formulated milk and tea/coffee, and these packs were distributed at night-time. However, for one establishment, cooked breakfasts were offered to women in the dining-hall with options of tea and toast too.

---

1 Please note as a safety warning: kettle cooking may potentially damage the kettle, and if doing this please unplug the kettle before removing food with a utensil.

> *Yes, and I think 'cos like this morning I had like a breakfast, like bacon and egg bun and then for dinner you can have whatever here, do you know what I mean so like a minced pie, you can have a brew, so when you go over you're like full and then I think I am not eating tonight, I am going to put loads of weight on panicking.*

Many women also tried home comforts that were infused with their home life and cultural backgrounds. In the case of this dish, it is based on this woman's Jamaican heritage — cornmeal porridge is a common dish served in Jamaica as a popular breakfast choice.

Cornmeal Porridge

> *I also make cornmeal porridge in my kettle.*
> *It's like a maize, like polenta. But you can*
> *make it like in a porridge. So, you boil the*
> *milk, add the polenta, cornmeal, keep stirring*
> *and stirring and stirring, add your sugar.*

In this, other recipes that have been influenced by Jamaican heritage have had two prominent ingredients from the island — callaloo and onions. Canteen ingredients like onions are easy to purchase and provide additional taste for women when making dishes from the kettle.

BANANA MAN LOUISE

Callaloo

Yes, with callaloo. So, you boil it in the kettle. Everything's the kettle, you have to boil it and then you mix it, but getting the salad from the kitchen is crucial because you get the onions, the peppers, the tomato and what's the other thing, the onions and stuff like that. And then obviously you can ... because sometimes I keep a little salad from Friday because you want the tomato. So, you want it in the food and then you want it on the side as well. So, my friend was just, like, she comes to me and is, like, 'Are you cooking today?' And I'm, like, 'I don't cook during the week, just on the weekends really when we get locked in early.'

Another key ingredient that has been easy to access and cook is noodles. Furthermore, noodles are also seen to be of value in the prison and are sometimes used as 'informal payment' in the prison economy (Gibson-Light, 2018). For those incarcerated, doing this is an act of resistance against capitalist practices dominated by the prison, and as a way to navigate the cost-of-living crisis. This was followed up by some of the women who spoke about the dire wages in prisons where they could not afford to buy any food:

There's some of us that can afford to do it. There's some of us that can't afford to do it because the wages are so crap in prison. Some people don't have people sending money in for them. So for me I just like to give, so me sharing my food with them, it's ... yeah.

Noodles Kettle Cooking

> *And the same with noodles as well. I sometimes keep my chicken; I save half my chicken and then Sunday evening with the noodles and with the salad. But there is always salad floating around here because some girls just want the egg, they don't want the salad.*

Other ingredients that were used included red beans, which was an option for many women that was readily available on the canteen. Red beans were used in many dishes including curries, chillies or even as a way to snack to combat long periods of hunger. However, despite the popularity of red beans, some of the women noted that the cost of a tin of beans had increased since the cost-of-living crisis

It's costing £10 for your tins of beans. And one tin of beans could only do about three people.

Curried Beans

In the kettle, if you do not have anything else No pasta, just a curry, with beans, yeah, and it was just nice, it was really, nice, it was different, red beans were in it, it was nice. And onions, tomatoes, just all different things, spices, it was nice.

CHOICE
ANGEL

Kettle Chow Mein

> *Yes, so I've got a spare kettle, so I sauté garlic and onion and chilli flakes, take that out, slice all the mushrooms, cook off all the mushrooms and slice the pepper, cook off the pepper, add the chow mein sauce, cook the noodles in a Tupperware, add it all together with the chow mein, done.*

Fish like mackerel is regarded as high value in the prison estate. Many of the women cooked mackerel to keep healthy or as a part of having more choice, with many of the women's testimonies including reference to, for example, eating mackerel and rice.

> *On the menu, it's just the same over weeks, different weeks. They'll do, for instance, pasta carbonara, lasagne, fish and chips on a Friday. That's quite okay, fish and chips. I don't mind that. They do a nice spring roll here, vegan spring roll. That, with the sweet chilli sauce, that's nice. I do eat that. Then, they'll do fish stuff... They do a variety of stuff but it's continuous. It's just that same stuff over and over. There's never anything new on the menu. It's just the same over, and over, and over, and over again.*

Mackerel Curry

> *Your basmati rice in your kettle for a bit and get make away curry powder. You just mix it in a bowl and keep adding hot water, stir it and then get your rice out, drain your rice. But you've got to put a plate over your bowl, drain your rice and then put it on a plate. And then you get your mackerel, put your mackerel in your curry, stir it all around and then pour it over.*

Another item bought from the canteen was cornflakes. Many women spoke about buying cornflakes or Coco Pops to alleviate hunger pains which many experienced during the evenings as dinners were quite early in the day.

CLOGGED PIPES

GUT
HEALTH
ANGEL

Cornflake 'Fucking Buns'

> *I've known people to be able to like, they like melt chocolate on the kettle and they make like cornflake fucking buns and shit like that.*

COLLAGE KAREN

Other Kettle Uses

Many of the women spoke about the use of kettle for cooking but many saw the importance of using the kettles for other domestic chores including soaking plates and making coffee.

> *Massively and I have a kettle in my room, so for example, I've got up and I've had a coffee before I've even been unlocked this morning, I'm up, and I'm able to do things, I can soak my plates if I need to, because the water is hot enough, yeah it makes a big difference actually. You can make some noodles late at night, if you're really hungry.*

Kettle cooking has been an important lens for examining cooking in prison, and this complements the next sections that explore social and cultural identities; and how women celebrate key events.

Taste of Home: Dreams of Social Cultural Identities

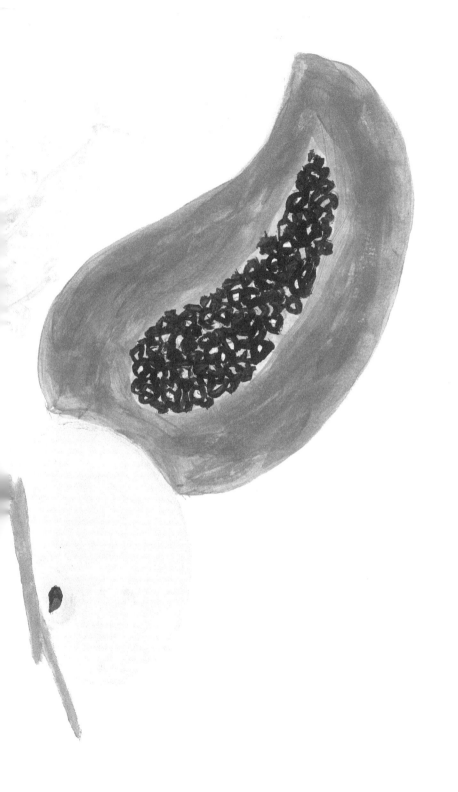

Previous Page:
Fruit Salad
Summer

Helping [my Jamaican Grandmother] with different things for different events and learning the different techniques and different dishes that I thought, well let me see what they've got and then I can incorporate what I know and what I've been taught with what they have and being able to provide for the women and give them some of, you know, the food that will give them life, give them energy so to speak.

Yes, at the table, it was always, very much sit at the table, have your dinner and then you go off. That was the way we liked to do it … Yes it was just nice to sit altogether and then you know, I don't know it was just something my parents always wanted to do eating at the table my mum always said it was better for digestion anyway, I don't know if that is actually true but [laughter].

Many of the women spoke about the dishes that connected them to memories and a sense of home, which they bought in to the prison. As Crawley (2004: 415) notes:

'Prisons are domestic in character precisely because they are places in which people have to live … In prisons, therefore, we find pet birds, family photographs, gossip and rumour, shopping lists for canteen purchases […] and so on'.

As such, people can bring aspects of their previous domestic lives into prison. Although not every incarcerated person has a home life which they would wish to recreate, attempts to bring aspects of the 'home' in prisons can be key to building a sense of normalcy, routine, and comfort, both for those who experienced this on the outside and those who did not. This can include decorating cells, wearing specific clothes, carrying out rituals and traditions such as watching certain television shows at certain times, or eating a roast dinner on a Sunday, and, of course, recreating dishes from home. In the women's prison estate, attending to the domestic elements of the prison experience are particularly crucial as women tend to be responsible for, and spend more time in, the domestic space.

Existing research on food practices in the community highlights a gendered pattern of food work whereby women retain much of the responsibility for everyday food work in families. For women, food has been recognised as a way in which they can construct themselves as recognisably womanly (DeVault, 1991) through cooking and caring for others. Mothers in prison may be experiencing emotions including loss and uncertainty (Baldwin, 2022). Cooking for others may be an important way of showing care and connecting with this part of the self. Aspects of social identity relating to gender and motherhood also intersect with that of being mothered, and the cultural and ethnic context in which this takes place.

Smoyer and Kjær Minke document how incarcerated women in Denmark attempt to construct 'hygge', a 'a cozy sense of belonging and warmth that is central to Scandinavian cultures' (2019:1) within the prison. They identified that food was a key part of this practice, both within the cell and the common areas of the prison, as it allowed them to eat, and to share 'cozy' food which reminded them of home. As cooking, eating and sharing food is a key way for incarcerated people, particularly women, to help recreate their domestic experiences, rituals and traditions within the prison, we have entitled this section 'Taste of Home'.

The dishes in this section range from main course to dessert and snacks, giving nutrition, comfort and a taste of home. They connect with identities outside of the prison, specific times and specific people that are important and memorable to them. These dishes are customised in the unique space in which they are prepared. As the dishes suggest, some women had access to a microwave, but this was not the case for all.

Consuming the dishes in prison, and sharing them with others, was an important practice for the women. This helped to recreate home through the sensory practices of handling ingredients, smelling the food cooking and sitting down to eat with others in a social setting. The recipes span various times of the day also — from main meals to comforting midnight snacks. They are held together by being domestic-inspired dishes prepared and consumed in the institutional setting of the prison. As well as being related to memories, connections to home were also aspirational and wanted for many women in prison.

Pumpkin Seed Fry

She [Susan — another woman in prison] used to cook spinach, like there's a Nigerian dish with spinach. Basically you know pumpkin seeds?

They dry them out and it has a white shell, like a grey and white shell. They peel that and then the actual white bit inside the seed they blend it in my culture, in Nigeria. And when they blend it, some people blend onions, like half an onion, and they mix it. And it goes into this little paste. The way they cook the stew is they get red, it has to be red, sweet peppers, tomatoes and onions and garlic, they blend that. You pour oil on the cooker, you pour it on, you put your Maggi seasonings or your all purpose. And when that cooks down, like about 20, 30 minutes, then you add the spinach. And if you're going to put fish in it you add fish. My mum used to get, they're selling it in Peckham, smoked prawns. They're dried, smoked prawns. My mum would soak them in water. Smoked fish, like they're hard and smoked. And she'd soak them in water and then she'd throw those in it. When the spinach was cooked, it doesn't take long, she'd add the fresh fish and the fresh prawns. Then she'd get the paste and put little balls in it and I'd have that with rice, I love it [...].

Many of the recipes used traditions from home to cook in prison, another woman spoke about a traditional Nigerian recipe called Moin Moin which is a bean pudding — and this woman used the resources in prisons to recreate this:

Moin Moin (Moi Moi)

And Moin Moin. I watched a programme once, I didn't realise, you know Portuguese people, and I noticed the other day as well, some Cubans, you know black-eyed beans, we soak them in water and then we blend them. With peppers or onions, red peppers and onions, and you season them with salt, whatever. And then you chop up onions, thin onions, and throw them. Then you fry them and it's like Akara. But instead of doing that, you don't put onions in it, you put a bit of sardine in it, any form of fish, it could be pilchard with tomato sauce. You break it into pieces, put it in it. And then some people have it plain, without, you put it in little containers and you steam them. And you put a boiled egg inside of it before you steam it. So it's just beans. But that's one of my favourites as well. They made that here for Black History Month.

Then other women spoke about trying to sustain memories of home life by buying food from the canteen and using the microwave.

Special Fried Rice

I do special fried rice … So, I'll cook the rice in the microwave with your peppers. We will get the chicken sausages or whatever sausages, bits of chicken, bits of beef. Everything gets cooked in the microwave separately and then —

Steaked Stew

And the ladies when I cook, they've never tasted food like that. A few weeks ago someone gave it to me as they were going, because when they're going home they don't want these tins, but I don't eat steaked stew. I was thinking, it's got a lot of fat in it, I've got a conscious thing about fat, I don't like fat. So I was thinking, I'm not going to eat that but I'm going to give it to someone. So one day a bunch of them were hungry and then I said, 'Okay, I've got this stew, do you guys eat that?' They said yes. But instead of cooking it down, because I'm very conscious about the fat in it, because someone had cooked it once for me and I was like, there's fat in it. So I was like, no, I'm not eating that. If you cook something down the fat cooks down. So I cut peppers and tomatoes and garlic, I seasoned it, put turmeric and garam masala and all purpose. And then I fried that in the micro with a bit of oil, fried it down for about 20 minutes. Then I poured the stew in and then I cooked the stew for about an hour … but because when I made it that day, they've went and now bought, there's another one there on the canteen, a beef stew with potatoes and carrots. I'm being serious, the officers were looking at me. I think one of the officers thought it was me. Because she came over and said, 'What are you cooking? It smells really nice.'

I said, 'Oh, it's stew.' She was like, 'Oh, where did you get the meat from?' I said, 'They bought it in the canteen, in a tin.' She was like, 'That's from the canteen?' I was like, 'Yes.' She said, 'Oh, what did you do to it?' So I told her what I did to it. Their one, I just cooked the same way, peppers and that, and I cooked down the tomatoes, because I use green tomatoes. Because I watched a programme once, you know Mexicans, they cook with green tomatoes and the green tomatoes are higher in vitamin C than a red tomato.

One of the favourites for women was, like university students, the traditional university pasta dish. It is based around pasta, tuna, mayonnaise, and a bit of cheese — this has been known to be cheap to buy and easy to make — and with the dinner provided at 4 pm and in some prisons, it was cold — this was a key dish that was filling for women to have at night-time.

University Pasta

On this occasion I did a student one, that I would have made when I was student. So, I had some mayonnaise, some onion, tuna, and cheese. Cheese that I'd saved from the weekend from something else, I get a little pot of cheese. I bought the tuna, bought the mayonnaise, I bought the onion, and I bought the pasta, so that was me, I financed that meal if you like. Chop the onion up, took the tuna out the tin, put it into the cooked pasta, once it was cooked. Put the mayonnaise in, stirred it, put the cheese on top, then put it back in to melt the cheese a little bit … It's not particularly nice, but I don't know … It was university one we made up, of things we had in the cupboards one time, a friend of mine, so I find it quite comforting …

Cheesecake is well-known in prison cooking — it was depicted in the television series, *Orange is the New Black*. Stearns (2019) identified that dessert and cakes in prison were key signifiers to gendered identities and it reinforced maternal and caregiving identities. We found that there were many representations of cheesecake including:

Oreo Cheesecake

> *And we make cheesecakes and they're literally better than outside … We crush up Oreos, and then we have to melt the butter, so we just put in hot water, like a square butter in like a plastic, so we melt the butter, crush up Oreos, mix it together to make a base, and then you can buy thick cream on the canteen, white chocolate, so you melt down the white chocolate in the kettle, but you just put a bowl on top of the kettle, and then you mix the cream and the chocolate together, pour it on and then sprinkle Oreo on top, so it's like a Oreo cheesecake. It's so nice.*

GRATER ON WHEELS
SIMRAN

Publisher's note: The editors made the artistic choice to use this piece on the book cover in a grater's more typical culinary orientation.

Microwave Cheesecake

> *But I mean we managed to have a cheesecake the other day, using the microwave. So you buy a can of condensed milk, pour that into a tub and obviously cook it in the microwave until it goes really, really sticky. Then my friend works in the kitchen, so she brought back some real butter and some soft cheese. Mix it all together. Then we melted chocolate, bought a packet of digestive biscuit, crushed them up but obviously melted the butter into them, put it all together, chucked it in the fridge, the next day we were loving life.*

Other than buying canteen snacks like chocolate or sweets, many women spoke about the need to make snacks that would also be a filling between the early dinners and the late lunches —

COLLAGE OF FOOD APRIL

Ice Cream

> *Even showed them how to make — you can*
> *make ice-cream if you had a freezer and I used to*
> *ask the staff, 'Oh, can I just borrow your freezer?'*
> *Because, obviously, they like me, I made ice-cream*
> *and put it in the freezer. Made ice-cream, easy.*

I: How? How?

R: So tinned thick cream. You know you get the Carnation, the thick cream?

I: Oh, yes, yes.

R: Thick cream and … what do I use? The thick cream and condensed milk, a little bit of vanilla essence, whip it up, you've got your ice-cream. Lovely too. One time I gave it to a staff member to taste and she was like, 'Hold on a minute, how did you get ice-cream in?' She goes, 'It tastes really good.' Trust me, thick cream and condensed milk.

Midnight Snacks

Ooh, that'd be telling [laughter]. No, I'm only joking. So, when we get the beef or chicken baguettes, it is already cooked, so what we will do is then we will chuck it all in with sauces. So, all the girls will say, 'Right, this is what we are going to cook.' We will get all the girls to order that chicken baguette from that day, we will get it off the baguette, scrape off whatever, wash it down, and recook it ... So, there's your chicken for the thing, and then the baguettes, we'll basically put cheese on that or summat, have a cheese toastie that night. But save the chicken for the proper meal the day after. Same again with the beef. Like you'll get a beef baguette, all of you, strip that back.

Celebrations in Prison

PREVIOUS PAGE:
CAKES GALORE
PENNI

Yes, we make cheesecakes ...

Well it really depends as a group. It really depends on which group I am in, because I've got a lot of friends in here and they are all very supportive over me. They are like we'll have Bridget [me] over this side ... We club together to share food ... I bring a lot, I bring stuff up onto the landing for extras and it will be Bridget 'Have you got this, Bridget have you got that?' I am like, 'Yes, I've got this, yes I've got that.'

Women often discussed baking and cooking for birthday celebrations and religious holidays like Eid or Christmas. Baking for birthdays was often a collective endeavour, with women contributing different ingredients that they had bought from the prison shop (also known as canteen). Sometimes, the ingredients were relatively expensive, given the generally low income of the women, and buying all the ingredients for a cake was often not an option. Sharing the cost and the effort in making a cake enabled the women to mark significant celebrations for each other.

Baking was a joy and a creative outlet for many women and could act as a way of building and maintaining friendships. One woman told us that her friend made special requests for her birthday and had wanted a cheesecake. Improvisation was key for this task, as she had to substitute cream cheese with Angel Delight (usually a liquid or powder mix which can make a mousse-like dessert).

When we were undertaking this research project, the effects of Covid-19 were still with us in a major way. Most of those serving sentences in prison had experienced more isolation from each other, spending most of their days in their cells in order to limit possible transmission of the virus. This sometimes took a toll on people's mental health, made worse by not having people to spend time with. As life began to improve during 2022 and beyond, some of the women reflected on time missed — the simple things like celebrating birthdays and similar celebrations. These had the benefit of bringing people together more, making up for lost time from the period of isolation during Covid-19:

> *We were all able as a group to celebrate together and it was nice sort of comfortable, we sang happy birthday and we'd all missed it because we hadn't been able to do it during Covid so it was nice once it had finished to be able to do that together because it's not the same doing it on your own or with just one or two people.*

Opportunities for sharing food also became more apparent. Sharing food has a practical benefit in team working, building relationships, often acting as an expression of trust and care towards one another. In prison, relationships with other women were often made stronger through food.

> *I've got a lot of friends in here and they are all very supportive over me. They are like we'll have Megan over our side, we'll have creativity there.*

And do you club together or do you share food or anything like that?

> *Oh we do, we do, I bring a lot, I bring stuff up onto the landing for extras and it will be 'Have you got this, Megan, have you got that?' I am like 'Yes, I've got this.'*

COLLAGE KERRY

Creativity and Resourcefulness

When it came to the actual dishes themselves, the women were extremely creative and resourceful. If you imagine only having very basic cooking materials available to you — perhaps only a kettle in your cell, or sometimes a shared microwave available in a more communal part of the prison wing or landing area — the women had to work with what they had to produce these dishes.

PINEAPPLE DAZE BECKY

PINK BIRTHDAY CAKE WITH CANDLES AUBREY

Rocky Road

I did a rocky road recently, melted the chocolate, broke up some biscuits, chopped up loads of marshmallows with Rice Krispies, and just mix it all in, let it set, because we have got a fridge. I did put it in the fridge for too long so it went a bit hard, but in this weather, it soon softened up. [laughter]. Um but someone on, what day was it, I think it was Sunday had made a crumble because she obviously saved the pears and apples and it was pear and apple crumble and we get sort of cereal bars every day, they are like oaty cereal bars, they just broke them up crumbled that on put it in the microwave with some custard, it was delicious, and we can get things like cinnamon and different spices on our canteen here, so then obviously when you make loads of things, or even if you like to put a little bit of chilli powder in your food, you can do that here, which is good.

Chocolate Cheesecake

You can buy jelly off the canteen; you can buy custard off the canteen and you can buy cream as well. We do a cheesecake now and again. So we get digestive biscuits, crush them in to look like ... so they're just all crushed and put them in the bottom of the tray. Then we have to use like cream. We get it all in the canteen. We use cream, a chocolate. What else? Butter. Then it's just like a cheesecake. Oh it's beautiful. Just a layer of chocolate on top with the cream, it's nice. We leave it in the fridge for an hour, yeah.

Angel Delight Cheesecake

> *We make cheesecakes and that, so, like, we crush digestive biscuits, or we put it in a big bowl and then we get Angel Delight put that over the top and then get chocolate buttons, put them on, and, like, Smarties and that. And, like, it was Sandy's and Patricia's [joint] birthday a few months ago, and we bought them Balconi cakes and we put icing on them and, like, decorated them with Maltesers and that …*

Some of the women spoke about coming together to celebrate Christmas, and the women spoke about cooking together to make a buffet.

Buffet Celebrations

We all chip in [contribute] with canteen and we all like put bits of food from our canteen in one big table. Somebody might make a cornflake cake, or somebody might make pasta or noodles. Anything really . . .

Another woman spoke about cooking chapatis together in the main kitchen via buying from the canteen as a way of celebrating an event together.

Yes, we all chip in each week with something and then myself and Patricia and Betty will go up to the main kitchen and even Charmaine as well that lives in No 38 . . . she will go up and she'll cook a curry and then she'll say, 'Cook your chapatis,' and the other night we went up there, we wanted to test out how to make onion bhajis but using cornflour just to see because sometimes we can get flour on the canteen and sometimes it's doesn't come and then sometimes cornflour comes, so we wanted to see how it worked and what we needed to . . . Yes, so we mashed down the chickpeas and chopped onions and potato and mashed them in, and then we put the cornflour in and then fried them in the oil, but they came out okay, I wouldn't say they were quite onion bhaji but they were good enough. They were tasty.

Chocolate Pudding in a Mug

> *You can make like a pud in a mug. So flour, hot chocolate powder, we can buy eggs because obviously the garden has got chickens, chuck in a microwave, done, thank you very much.*

fear of food

I've been inside five years to long,
The food inside just really wrong,
I can't eat the food it makes me Fat,
I have to admit I aint Greatful for that,
I eat one meal, I know it aint Great,
I Live in fear that i might Gain weight
maybe one day this Feeling will end,
up until then my Fat is my Friend.

FEAR OF FOOD MELISSA

CELEBRATORY CAKE PRECIOUS

Carrot Cake

Women spoke about the food they would like to cook and consume when they are released, and this woman spoke about the plans in going back home and the importance of carrot cake. As Mary said:

> Yes, yes (laughter) yes mum's already said I am making a carrot cake for when I come home ... so thanks by the mum (Laughing at the fact that she has to cook). Yes this is my favourite — I do love carrot cake. This is also my Mum and Dad's favourite ... especially this time of year I do apple, blackberry, carrot and sultana cake and that's really nice. And I do it with oat milk so it gives it that sort of nutty taste as well. Yes ... So, when I did the International Women's Day last week, I did five flavours, I did banana, chocolate, vanilla, lemon and carrot. So yes, a lot of people loved the ... to be honest, people loved all of them but the ones I heard the most about were the carrot and banana, they loved them.

I: I might tap you up for the recipe as well because I love carrot cake.

R: Yes, I do, carrot cake and banana, I love it but with my banana one, I'll put dark chocolate chips in to give it a sort of ... oh it's so nice.

I: Pecans in the carrot cake as well.

R: Yes, pecans in the carrot cake is nice.

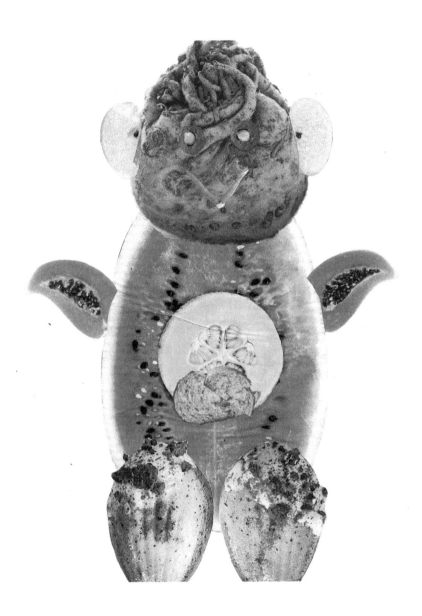

FRUIT 'MONKEY' MONTANA

Microwave Birthday Cake

> *I had a birthday when I was in prison and I had a cake made for me, all microwave made, made out of Biscoff biscuits and butter, and they made the icing filling with yoghurts, fresh blueberries and butter I think it was.*

BEACH DREAM ANDREA

HAPPY MEAL LEAH

Concluding Thoughts

Testimonies from women spoke about the narratives of the dishes that were created to help the women feel empowered but to also resist the hostile tensions of the prison. As a result, many of these dishes offered a chance to escape realities and to use memories as a way to move forward and to aspire to once the women were released. The kettle has been a notable method of cooking, and whilst these testimonies have come from women in prison, the use of kettles has also been evidenced in men's prisons, and overseas in countries like the United States, Australia, and Canada. Many of the women made these dishes with 'love', dedication and commitment to dishes that were connected to cultural and home life. Women's identities in prison are always connected to the relationships outside, and the dishes narrated are an example of how women try to find ways to recreate home life.

The dishes in this book represent ways women become creative in times of adversity. It enables the reader to see that women use the resources around them to find methods to cook that signal ways to identify with the outside world. Also, these dishes tell a narrative about the friendships that are formed between women in the prison and provide small examples of feeling a sense of closeness with others. These bonds are vital, especially at the time when these testimonies were created, when the women were still in the midst of heavy restrictions in the prison due to the pandemic. So, for a long period of time, many women were in isolation for up to 23 hours a day in their cells and had to eat by themselves. The ideas of cooking together were to a degree incidences of exceptions, and this is why is it significant to make a 'song and dance' about the importance of cooking together. Further to this, the use of cooking can also contribute to the development of independent living skills that will help in the long run for when many women are released. Lastly, the use of these dishes has provided a way to open conversations about sensory practices including the role of taste, smell, sight, and the dialogue surrounding food.

Campaign for Change

We wanted to make this book as a call for a 'campaign for change' to improve the quality of food in prisons. The discussions have been solely focused on women; however, we can argue to some extent that there needs to be wider change across the prison system for both men and women on the budget, quality, and value placed on food. These dishes give an insight into the details of prison life, and we wanted to see if there are ways we can use this book to recommend changes. Inspired by the women's narratives, we would like to improve the quality of food and to do this, we would advocate for the following changes:

1. Raise public awareness about the importance of food in prisons, and to change perceptions around ideas that food is equated to forms of punishment.
2. Increase the prison food budget to enable the dietary and cultural needs for women in prison to be met.
3. Enhance spaces and resources for women to cook in prison, and to encourage cooking together to address cultural and dietary needs.
4. Increase partnerships between prisons and other agencies that will work to improve the quality of food in prison, including voluntary organizations.

TEA GINGER GARLIC RED ONION PEAN

CHICKPEAS KIDNEY BEANS SWEETCORN

SILENCE HOPELESSNESS ENDLESSN

REALITY TV ITVBE DATES PASTA FI

SUDOKU CROSSWORDS DISTRACTION

consumption consump

I AM WHAT I EAT

ART CYNACLE

I

LOVE

H AM

I EAT

SEE

LISTEN

READ

TASTE

TOUCH

EAT AWAKE

HAT I TOUCH I AM

consumption consumption

consumption consumption

WHAT I ALLOW

FABRICATIONS

Cauliflower Milk

Green Peas

carrots

Broccoli

PAST PRESENT

HISTORY FUTURE

CRYPTOCURRENCY FRUSTRATION

DONATIONS

LIFE PLUMS OFF THE SHELF TIME

RAISINS SUNFLOWER SEEDS FOUR SEED MIX WATER MINT GREEN

CONSUM

LE A BREAK BBC GOOD FOOD country

SWEET POTATO ALTERED FREEDOM

TION FINE LINER PEAS CHARCOAL BIRO

EE ART LITERATURE RICE POTATOES

UCUMBER SPRING ONIONS FETA OATS

TTER MARMITE BUTTER CHEESE BREAD NICE

US DVDS CDS DREAMS HARSH WORDS

EANS EGGS HASH BROWNS Melancholy

ESLAW PINEAPPLE NOODLES MUSTARD

Watermelon Bananas BARRIERS

nsumption consumption

WHAT I READ I AM

ATIVE HERE

I AM

JOY

AM WHAT I HEAR I

FULL EMPTY AL

MY

I AM WHAT I SPEAK I

READ

TASTE

TOUCH

EAT

 consumption consumption consumption consumption

CRISPIES CHOCOLATE ORANGES OLIVES BELL PEPPERS

ISOLATION SOLITUDE MUSHROOMS APRICOTS DATES

NOSTALGIA HOPE CHAOS DISORDER POETRY

HOT PEPPER SAUCE SALAD CREAM BROWN SAUCE

CHICKEN MUESLI BLUEBERRIES KIWI FRUIT

Ideas KOESTLER OUTREACH

SWEET CHILI SAUCE CORIANDER SMA

CODEWORD PUZZLES INSIDE TIMES

HARD KNOCKS CLASSICAL MUSIC YOGA

CUSTARD CREAMS CAKE APPLES PEAR

AVOCADO BEETROOT FETA LETTUCE T

I Am Katie

References

Baldwin, L (2022), *Mothers In and After Prison*, Sherfield on Loddon: Waterside Press.

Baroness Corston (2007), The Corston Report: The need for a distinct radically different, visibly led strategic proportionate holistic woman-centred integrated approach. Corston report — review of women with vulnerabilities in the Criminal Justice System, asdan.org.uk

Crawley, E (2004), Emotion and Performance: Prison Officers and the Presentation of the Self, *Punishment and Society,* 6(4): 411–427.

DeVault, M (1991), *Feeding the Family: The Social Organisation of Caring as Gendered Work*, Chicago: University of Chicago Press.

Gibson-Light, M (2018), Ramen Politics: Informal Money and Logics of Resistance in the Contemporary American Prison, *Qualitative Sociology,* 41(2): 199–220.

UK Government (2024), Prison Population Figures: 2024, www.gov.uk/government/publications/prison-population-figures-2024

HMIP (2016), Life in Prison: Food. A findings paper by HM Inspectorate of prisons. https://www.justiceinspectorates.gov.uk/hmiprisons/wp-content/uploads/sites/4/2016/09/Life-in-prison-Food-Web-2016.pdf

Smoyer, A and Kjær Minke, L (2019), Hygge: Food and the Construction of Safety Among Incarcerated Women, *Appetite,* 141: 104319.

The Guardian (2024), Cost of Eating Crisis: Price of school lunches up by a third in parts of England.

Acknowledgments

Thank you to everyone who has helped make this book come alive. A special thanks to Erika Flowers, the artist, who facilitated the art workshops where the artwork showcased in this book was produced. Thank you to Claire Warrington for her valuable contribution to the project and fieldwork on which this book is based. We appreciate the support of prison staff in facilitating the fieldwork. Thanks to Koestler Arts for their pivotal roles in the success of the 'On my Plate' exhibition at South Hill Park at which the art in this book was showcased. Lastly, sincere thanks to the women whose voices and artwork made this book.

August 2024

Maria Adams
Jon Garland
Vicki Harman
Daniel McCarthy
Erin Power
Talitha Brown

Index

Milton Keynes UK
Ingram Content Group UK Ltd.
UKHW052146190924
448461UK00018B/264

9 781914 603495